FOOD-BORNE ILLNESSES

FOOD-BORNE ILLNESSES

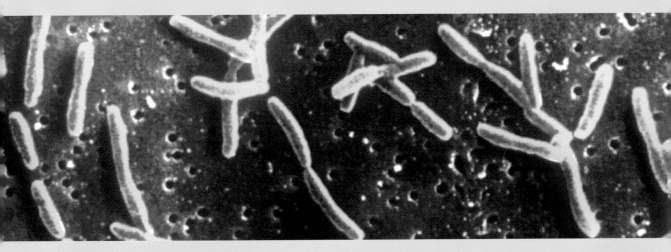

Ruth Bjorklund

Marshall Cavendish
Benchmark
New York

Special thanks to Tony, Ash, and Ms. Fulgham

Marshall Cavendish Benchmark
99 White Plains Road
Tarrytown, New York 10591-9001
www.marshallcavendish.us

This book is not intended for use as a substitute for advice, consultation, or treatment by a licensed medical practitioner. The reader is advised that no action of a medical nature should be taken without consultation with a licensed medical practitioner, including action that may seem to be indicated by the contents of this work, since individual circumstances vary and medical standards, knowledge, and practices change with time. The publisher, author, and medical consultants disclaim all liability and cannot be held responsible for any problems that may arise from use of this book.

Library of Congress Cataloging-in-Publication Data

Bjorklund, Ruth.
  Food-borne illnesses / by Ruth Bjorklund.— 1st ed.
      p. cm. — (Health alert)
  Summary: "Discusses food-borne illnesses and their effects on people and society"—Provided by publisher.
  Includes index.
  ISBN 0-7614-1917-9
  1. Foodborne diseases—Juvenile literature. I. Title. II. Series: Health alert (Benchmark Books)

  RA601.5.B57 2005
  615.9'54—dc22   2005005786

Front cover: *E. coli*
Title page: *Campylobacter*

Photo research by Candlepants, Inc.
Front cover: Manfred Kage/Peter Arnold Inc.
The photographs in this book are used by permission and through the courtesy of: *Photo Researchers, Inc:* VEM, 3, 17; Jane Shemilt, 8; Chris Bjornberg, 11; Science Photo Library / John Bavosi, 12; BURGER, 15; Science Photo Library / CNRI, 18; Eye of Science, 22; Bill Bachman, 25; Science Photo Library / Dr. Jeremy Bygess, 29; Richard T. Nowitz, 37; Dr. Gary Gaugler, 40; Science Photo Library / Mark Clarke, 43. *Visuals Unlimited:* Dr. Dennis Kunkel, 23. *Art Resource:* Eric Lessing, 27. *Corbis:* 30; Bettmann, 35. *Envision:* 49. *PictureQuest:* Frank Siteman, 52. *Visuals Unlimited:* Dr. Dennis Kunkel, 23.

Printed in China
6 5 4 3 2 1

CONTENTS

1

WHAT IS IT LIKE TO HAVE A FOOD-BORNE ILLNESS?

"I've had broken bones, gone through surgery, and once, I was even hit by a speeding car while riding my bicycle, but none of that misery compares *in the least* to the time I had food poisoning," declares Tony, a student from California.

The day his illness began started out like any other day. Tony, a seventh grader at the time, had gone to school. But by lunchtime, he felt uneasy. His stomach ached, his head hurt, and he felt like he was going to vomit. He went home early and went to bed. Before long, he woke up and dashed to the bathroom and vomited. After that, he felt better. He even helped his mother with a craft project for awhile.

But the **nausea** returned, worse this time. The cramping feeling in his stomach made him curl up in pain. Four hours after he had come home from school, he vomited again. His mother called the school. No one else reported being sick. What had Tony eaten that no one else had? He remembers a cherry pie from a vending machine that he had eaten the day before. It had tasted a little strange, but Tony did not think that would be a problem.

Tony's father was a doctor. When he came home that night, Tony's father told him he would be alright and should just stay in bed. For the next three days, Tony vomited every four hours, around the clock. He recalls, "My stomachache was horrendous! I was so thirsty, my lips were cracked. But whenever I drank any water, I threw up. And each time I did, I'd tell myself, 'Thank goodness—that's the last time!'"

But it was not. By the fourth day, Tony's stomach ached beyond belief. Every two hours, he vomited violently. He could barely breathe. He was only able to lie moaning, on his bed. By the fifth day, his father gave him some medicine to stop the vomiting. But it did not help.

Day six, day seven, and day eight went by. Tony was exhausted. He vomited every hour, twenty-four times a day. "My stomach muscles and my ribs felt like someone had sliced me with a knife!" He could not walk. When he had to leave his bed to use the bathroom, he crawled on his hands and knees.

Improperly stored foods—such as meat—can cause food-borne illnesses. Never store raw and cooked meat together and always cover foods to keep them from spoiling.

Tony's father felt that it was a long-lasting "stomach flu," and that Tony should be over it soon. But he decided that if it went on for another day, Tony needed to go the hospital.

On the ninth day, to everyone's relief, Tony was a little better. He vomited less often. He could drink a little water and keep it down. He even was able to nibble on a cracker. But, during those nine, long days, Tony had lost 15 pounds— nearly 15 percent of his entire weight. "I never want to experience anything like that ever, ever again," he says.

His father now believes that Tony had eaten food contaminated with a deadly type of *E. coli* **bacteria.** Today, Tony is careful about what he eats. "If the food in the refrigerator isn't cold enough, if cooked food isn't hot enough, if the kitchen or restaurant or anyone who works there looks unclean, I don't eat. I examine everything. I take no chances!"

2

WHAT IS A FOOD-BORNE ILLNESS?

A food-borne illness occurs when a person becomes ill after eating or drinking **contaminated** foods or beverages. Nothing that we eat or drink is completely pure, and many **microorganisms** live in the foods and beverages that we consume. Microorganisms, or **microbes**, are tiny organisms such as bacteria, **fungi**, **viruses,** and **parasites** that exist in our bodies as well as in plants, animals, food, water, air, and soil. Many of these microbes do us no harm, and some "friendly" ones are necessary for a healthy body, but other microbes can cause infections that lead to serious, or even fatal, illness. Additionally, there are harmful chemicals and other substances in food that can cause a food-borne illness.

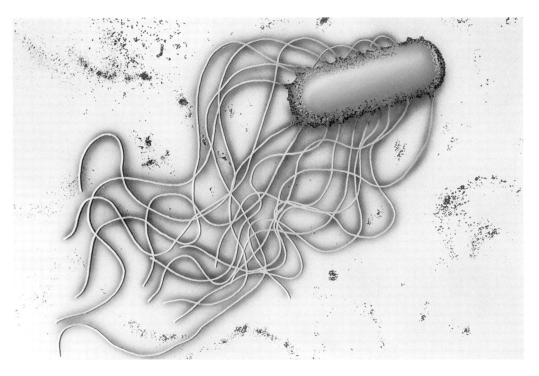

Salmonella bacteria can cause food poisoning, blood poisoning, and typhoid fever.

THE DIGESTIVE SYSTEM

There are many different **symptoms** linked to food-borne diseases, but most begin by infecting the gastrointestinal tract in the human body. The gastrointestinal tract is made up of the mouth, **esophagus**, stomach, and **intestines** and is part of the digestive system. The digestive system is the group of organs that take in food, process it to absorb **nutrients** and to make energy, and remove the waste from the body. The digestive system includes the mouth, esophagus, stomach, **liver,** pancreas, small intestine, large intestine, rectum, and anus. It is aided by parts of other systems, such as the nervous system (which involves the brain, spinal cord, and nerves), lymphatic system (a network that distributes lymph, a disease-fighting fluid, throughout the body), the circulatory system (how blood moves around the body), and the muscular system.

When people eat, the food consumed does not supply nourishment right away. The body must first digest the food. Digestion is the process that breaks food into a simpler form that can be used by the body for nourishment, energy, and growth. Digestion begins in the mouth where teeth grind and soften food. Enzymes, which are special chemicals produced by the body, begin breaking down food in the mouth. After swallowing, the food travels down the esophagus, a 10-inch long tube that empties into the stomach. Muscles in the

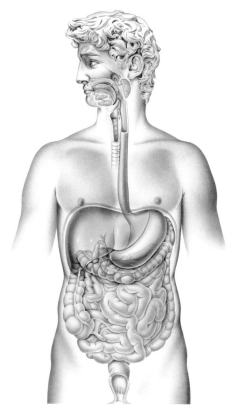

The digestive system processes most food in about 24 hours.

esophagus begin a rhythm of tightening and relaxing to squeeze the food and push it downward. This movement is called **peristalsis.** Peristalsis also prevents food from going the wrong way. Once the food passes through the esophagus and the opening to the stomach, digestion resumes.

The stomach is a muscular sac that expands to hold food. When food is present, the stomach contracts every twenty seconds and mixes the food with gastric juices. These juices include water, hydrochloric acid, an enzyme called **pepsin,** and mucus. The pepsin breaks down **proteins** in food. Hydrochloric acid is a powerful chemical that breaks down matter. Outside of the stomach, hydrochloric acid can burn a hole through a piece of metal in just moments. But inside the stomach, the acid aids the pepsin and works to kill harmful microbes in the food. Hydrochloric acid does not burn through the stomach and damage internal organs because of mucus. The stomach lining produces mucus to protect the organs from the acid.

After the food leaves the stomach, it moves into the small intestine. The small intestine is a folded, winding tube, about 1 inch in diameter and, when stretched out, about 20 feet long. Food moves through the small intestine over a period of three to five hours, pushed along by peristalsis. Different organs secrete—or squirt—fluids into the small intestine to aid digestion. The pancreas secretes different enzymes into the small intestine while the liver secretes a fluid called bile. The enzymes and bile break down food and turn it into nutrients that the body can use. Other enzymes found in the intestinal walls also help the process. Lining the walls are millions of tiny projections called villi. Villi transfer digested food to the lymphatic system and the bloodstream. In turn, the blood and lymph (a clear, disease-fighting body fluid) distribute nourishment throughout the body.

Next, undigested food and extra digestive juices—which can be called the "waste"—move to the large intestine, a U-shaped tube 2.5 inches wide and about 6 feet long. This undigested waste remains in the large intestine for up to 24 hours. During that time, the large intestine absorbs water from the waste—almost 1.5 gallons each day. Friendly bacteria work inside the large intestine to break down some of the waste into vitamins for use by the body. Once this process ends, the waste move to the rectum where it is stored until muscles in the rectum contract and move the waste—in the form of **feces** or stool—through the anus and out of the body.

COMMON SYMPTOMS

Scientists, researchers, and health-care workers have described more than 250 food-borne illnesses. However, most food-borne illnesses share similar symptoms. Common first symptoms are nausea, vomiting, abdominal cramps, and **diarrhea.** Nausea is an uneasy sensation in the stomach that may develop into an intense urge to vomit. Vomiting occurs when the stomach becomes irritated. Nerves—fibers that send and receive sensory information-send messages to the part of the brain that stimulates vomiting. The brain responds by sending messages that cause peristalsis to reverse, forcing the contents of the stomach up the esophagus and out through the mouth. Abdominal cramps are a painful clenching of the muscles that surround the stomach and intestines. (The abdomen is the part of the body between the chest and

Most people need at least 7-10 days to recover from a food-borne illness.

the hips.) Diarrhea is a condition that develops when the mucus lining of the intestines becomes irritated. Muscles push the undigested food through the intestines rapidly. This interferes with the large intestine's ability to absorb liquids. When the body excretes the feces, it is watery and acidic.

While all of these symptoms are uncomfortable and unpleasant, they are actually very helpful. Vomiting, abdominal cramping, and diarrhea are healthy responses to a gastrointestinal infection. This combination of symptoms is the body's way of ridding itself of harmful microbes as quickly as possible.

TYPES OF FOOD-BORNE MICROORGANISMS

Food-borne illnesses are caused by a wide variety of harmful microbes and chemicals. The most well known bacteria that cause food-borne diseases are certain types, or strains, of *Campylobacter, Salmonella, Listeria, Shigella, Clostridium,* and *E. coli.* The most common disease-causing viruses found in food are **noroviruses** and **Hepatitis A.** Harmful species— or types—of certain microorganisms found in food include: **Toxoplasma,** *Trichinella,* and *Giardia.* In addition, there are other types of substances that cause food-borne illnesses: fungi, such as poisonous mushrooms and certain cheese molds, agricultural pesticides, and toxic metals such as mercury and lead.

Bacteria and Viruses

The most common bacterium ("bacterium" is singular for "bacteria") to cause a food-borne illness is *Campylobacter*. This microbe lives in the intestines of birds. Most raw poultry meat contains *Campylobacter*. The bacteria are usually killed by heat when the meat is cooked. But when all the bacteria are not destroyed—such as when a person eats undercooked chicken—*Campylobacter* can cause an infection leading to **fever,** diarrhea, and abdominal cramps. Serious infections can leave a person permanently disabled with **chronic** pain, paralysis, or a nervous system disease called **Guillain-Barre syndrome**.

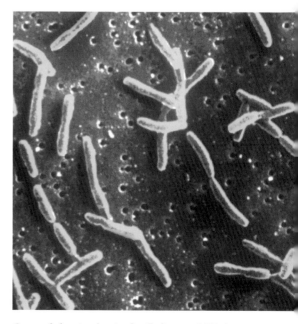

Another common food-borne illness is salmonellosis, which is caused by *Salmonella* bacteria that live in the intestines of humans, birds, and other animals. Foods that carry the bacteria are beef, poultry,

Campylobacter **bacteria thrive at 107 degrees Fahrenheit.**

Botulism is a very dangerous food-borne illness. If left untreated, the illness may be fatal.

milk, eggs, and vegetables. The infection can be passed along by under-cooked foods, unpasteurized milk and juice (**pasteurization** is a heat process that kills **germs**), or by food that is handled by an infected person with unwashed hands. Salmonellosis causes fever, vomiting, diarrhea, and abdominal cramps, especially in those with weak **immune systems** (the body system that fights disease and illness), such as infants, young children, elderly persons, and people with ongoing illnesses.

Listeriosis is a serious infection caused by eating food contaminated with a strain of bacteria called *Listeria*. This bacteria lives in soil and water. The bacterium can pass to plants and animals. Foods that can contain the bacteria are uncooked meats and vegetables, and unpasteurized milk, fruit juice, and cheese. Most healthy adults who consume

Listeria-infected foods do not become seriously ill, but pregnant women, newborns, and adults in fragile health can become gravely, or even fatally ill. A person with listeriosis has fever, muscle aches, and sometimes nausea and diarrhea. The infection can also spread to the nervous system, causing headaches, confusion, loss of balance, and **seizures.**

Botulism is the name of the disease caused by a strain of the bacterium *Clostridium*. Unlike many other disease-causing microbes, the bacterium *Clostridium* is not harmful in itself, but it makes a **toxin** (a poisonous substance) that affects the human nervous system. Just the tiniest amount of botulism is extremely dangerous. The toxin develops where there is little or no oxygen, such as in sealed, air-tight containers that have been improperly prepared or carelessly stored. (In other non-food-related cases, botulism can be caused when *Clostridium* infects wounds.)

Infections used to occur more frequently when people improperly canned foods at home. Today, most people do not can foods at home, but contamination can sometimes occur in food prepared in plants or factories. Infants under one year old are at risk of developing botulism if they are fed honey containing the bacteria. Botulism attacks the nervous system, causing blurred vision, drooping eyelids, slurred speech,

Mad Cow Disease

Mad cow disease is a disease that strikes cattle. The scientific name for the disease is bovine spongiform encephalopathy (BSE). BSE is caused by a deformed protein, called a prion, that slowly multiplies in the brain, eyes, and nervous system of cattle. When cattle are infected, they become weak, confused, and die.

Other animals can develop a disease similar to BSE, including humans. The human disease is called Creutzfeldt-Jakob disease (CJD). Worldwide, CJD strikes one person in a million. It is usually a disease that runs in families. But a small **outbreak** of a new form of the disease occurred in Great Britain in 1996. It was discovered that many British cattle herds were infected with BSE. Scientists believed the new cases of CJD were caused by people eating beef from BSE-infected cows. Other European countries also reported new cases of CJD.

Scientists and agricultural researchers have been studying the disease, its cause, and its possible spread to humans. Governments around the world have put in place strict new regulations concerning the health of beef cattle. At this time, there is no cure for the disease. But, the risk of developing CJD from a food-borne source is extremely small. The best prevention is to not eat cow brains or processed beef, which may include organ meats or bits of ground up nerve, such as lunch meats or hot dogs, from countries where BSE has been found in cattle.

difficulty swallowing, dry mouth, and muscle weakness. If left untreated, it can lead to death.

Food-borne illnesses caused by *E. coli* bacteria are a growing problem. There are hundreds of strains of *E. coli* that live in the intestines of healthy humans and other animals. One strain, however, called *E. coli* O157:H7 produces a powerful toxin and can cause serious illness. Most infections are developed when a person eats under-cooked ground beef, or swallows contaminated, unpasteurized milk or juice. The toxin has also been found on bean sprouts, lettuce, and cured meats. People who are infected with *E. coli* can pass the bacteria along to others, if they do not wash their hands. People who become sick with *E. coli* suffer nausea, vomiting, bloody diarrhea, **dehydration**, and sometimes kidney failure. Young people, elderly people, and people with weak immune systems who become infected with *E. coli* are at risk of permanent nerve damage, kidney disease, or death.

People can develop a food-borne illness caused by viruses such as noroviruses and the Hepatitis A virus. These viruses do not live in foods, but become attached to food when it has been handled by people who are infected. Both infections cause vomiting, nausea, diarrhea, and cramps. A norovirus infection lasts under a week, but a Hepatitis A infection affects the liver and can last for months. A person with Hepatitis A will also experience a yellowing of the skin and eyes, called jaundice.

Microscopic Parasites

Microscopic parasite infections are another form of food-borne illnesses. Trichinosis is a disease caused by eating raw or under-cooked meat of infected animals. Animals become

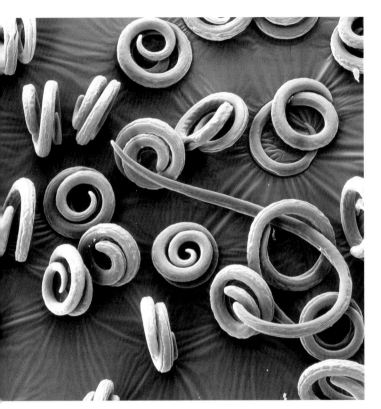

Immature *Trichinella* worms curl up and imbed themselves in the muscles of infected mammals. This is a magnified photograph of *Trichinella* on pork meat.

infected by eating raw meat containing the larvae (a juvenile stage of growth in an animal that has left its egg but is not fully developed) of a worm called *Trichinella*. Pork meat can sometimes contain trichinosis larvae, but the larvae are more often present in wild game such as seal, walrus, or bear. Heat will kill the larvae, but if meat is under-cooked, the larvae will survive.

Once a person eats the larvae, stomach acids break the outer shell of the larvae, and release the worm. The first symptoms of trichinosis are nausea, diarrhea, vomiting, fatigue, fever, and abdominal cramps. Headaches, eye swelling, and muscle pains often follow. The infection can last for six months. Serious infections affect the muscles, including the heart. If the illness goes untreated, there is risk of death.

A less invasive parasite, but far more common, is *Giardia*. *Giardia* larvae also have a very hard shell and can survive outside a **host** body for long periods of time. The *Giardia* parasite lives in the intestines of humans and other animals. It is spread in the feces of an infected person or animal and can be found all over the world in soil, food, water, or contaminated surfaces such as a bathroom counter. Generally, humans become infected when swallowing water containing the parasite. Symptoms can last up to two months and include nausea, diarrhea, and stomach cramps.

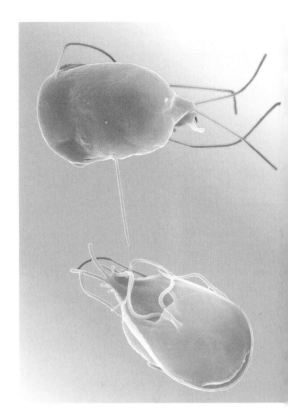

"Traveler's diarrhea" is usually caused by *Giardia*.

A food-borne illness called amoebic dysentery is caused by parasites called amoebae. Amoebae can be found in food or drink that have been improperly washed, stored, or heated. The most dangerous cases of amoebic dysentery occur in warm, tropical climates. After a person eats food infected with harmful amoebae, such as vegetables washed in contaminated water, he or she may not know for some time that an infection has happened. Symptoms of a mild case of amoebic dysentery are cramping and diarrhea. But in the most severe cases, the amoebae will attack the intestines of an infected person and pass through to the bloodstream, spreading to crucial organs. Because the amoebae live inside of a hard shell called a cyst, it can be difficult to treat. Serious amoebic dysentery causes severe vomiting and bloody diarrhea and large cysts can form in the liver or kidneys. A person who does not practice good hygiene at all times can spread the disease to others.

Other Causes

Other toxins and poisonous chemicals can cause food-borne illness. People can get sick from eating foods that contain **pesticides** used to kill insects and protect crops. Many mushrooms are poisonous, and food poisoning occurs when people mistakenly pick and eat wild mushrooms that are not safe. Fish and seafood also can contain poisonous substances, including bacteria, viruses, neurotoxins (toxins that damage the nervous system), heavy metals such as mercury, and dangerous concentrations of chemicals such as dioxin. (Dioxin is a toxic by-product of the manufacture of plastics and chemicals.)

Anyone, anywhere in the world can develop a food-borne illness. The Centers for Disease Control, often referred to as the CDC, is a United States government agency dedicated to tracking and studying infectious diseases, as well as distributing information about them. The CDC reports that an estimated 76 million Americans suffer from food-borne illnesses each year. More than 325,000 are hospitalized, and approximately 5,000 die each year as a result of food-borne illnesses. The World Health Organization (WHO) reports that more than 1.5 billion people worldwide suffer a food-borne illness, and more than 2 million people die from one each year, most of them children. Throughout the world, governments are making every effort to improve food safety for their citizens.

Red tides are a rapid growth of algae. Humans who eat shellfish that have fed on the algae can suffer serious poisoning and even death.

3

THE HISTORY OF FOOD-BORNE ILLNESSES

Microbes have been on Earth for billions of years. These tiny organisms live in the bodies of humans and other animals, as well as in plants, soil, water, and air. Most are harmless. But some are a threat to human life and health.

Scientists say that prehistoric people were very healthy. They hunted wild animals for food and gathered wild plants, fruits, and nuts. If certain plants or animals made people sick, they did not eat them again. When clean water was not available, they moved away. Being nomads, meaning that they moved from place to place in search of food, early humans could leave their dirty messes behind them and relocate to new, unsoiled settings. This often prevented waste from contaminating their food and homes.

But, starting around 10,000 to 12,000 BCE, humans began

settling down. They started
to farm crops and raise
animals. They also lived in
villages, and stayed close to
a common water supply.
Living side by side with
animals as well as near their
own wastes, the early humans
began suffering from new
diseases. Without knowing
the risk, humans allowed their
wastes to pollute the water.
The farmers also spread the
wastes, in the form of manure,

Many early civilizations separated drinking water from human waste, but did not understand the link between waste and disease.

on the ground as fertilizer to help the crops grow. All of
these activities exposed early humans to greater and greater
amounts of disease-causing germs.

As civilizations developed, many ancient societies, such as
in China, Crete, India, Egypt, Rome, Pakistan, and Great
Britain, made an effort to keep their food and water supplies
clean and safe. In 2700 to 2000 BCE, many of these societies
built water pipes and basic sewers, to separate fresh water
from dirty water. In Egypt, the twelfth century Jewish doctor

Maimonides advised people saying, "As for food of irregular taste such as bitter food, acid, sour, and the like, and any food giving off a bad odor, nothing should be partaken of them [eaten] without prior examination of their reliability." People learned to protect and preserve foods with salt, natural chemicals, dry heat, ice, and smoke. Romans carried ice from the Alps Mountains down to the lowlands to store food longer.

But cases of food-borne illnesses still increased. Wealthy people and royalty often had personal food tasters who sampled foods to test for toxins. During the Middle Ages (476 CE to 1453), many people in northern Europe were stricken with a food-borne disease called ergotism. It caused mental confusion, muscle spasms, gangrene (the death of body tissue), and sometimes death. Ergotism is now known to be caused by a fungus that grows on rye wheat in cold, wet climates. Although no one understood the link between the fungus and the disease at the time, in 1202, King John of England declared it against the law for bakers to prepare bread with impure ingredients. People were aware that molds, parasites, and other imperfections spoiled their food. But they did not yet know that tiny microbes, invisible to the eye, were multiplying all around them and causing infectious disease.

DISCOVERY

The first person to report seeing microbes under a microscope was an Englishman named Robert Hooke, in 1665. The lenses of his microscope were weak, and though he could detect fungi, he was not able to see bacteria. Later, in 1668, a Dutch cloth merchant named Anton van Leeuwenhoek developed a stronger microscope to examine cloth he was buying. His microscope's lenses were so powerful that he was able to see tiny organisms that we now know as bacteria.

At the time, he called them "little animalcules." Important people, including the Tsar of Russia and members of European royalty, flocked to Leeuwenhoek's laboratory to see these creatures. Leeuwenhoek also looked at different substances under his microscope and found many more tiny organisms. He

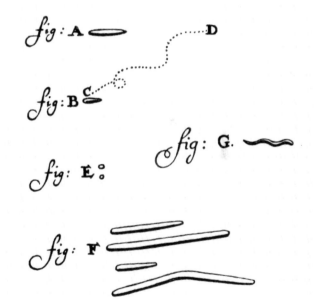

Leeuwenhoek's drawings of "animalcules."

even drew many illustrations of what he saw. (Present-day scientists have found that his illustrations are very close to some of the details they can now see with modern magnifying equipment.)

But it was not until two hundred years later that anyone realized the true importance of Leeuwenhoek's discovery. In 1857, a French chemist named Louis Pasteur developed what is called the "Germ Theory of Disease." Pasteur was the first to report that living viruses, bacteria, fungi, and other microbes, or germs, were responsible for diseases in plants and animals. Furthermore, his experiments showed that many harmful germs could be killed by heat. In 1857, sailors in the French navy were abandoning their ships because the wine stowed onboard had gone bad. Napoleon III, the Emperor of France, asked Pasteur to help. In his lab, Pasteur discovered that if he heated the wine to a certain temperature, most of the harmful germs would die. After heating the wine, he kept it

Louis Pasteur is often called the "Father of Microbiology."

cool. Chilling prevented any leftover germs from multiplying and spoiling the wine. Today, this process is used worldwide to preserve foods such as milk, eggs, and juice. It is called pasteurization.

Several inventions led to another important development in food safety—refrigeration. As early as prehistoric times, people learned that they could preserve food by keeping it cool in snow, in cold water, or in caves. Later, during the Middle Ages, the French discovered a way to add chemicals, such as sodium nitrate, to water to keep it cold. Most societies learned how to make and store blocks of ice, and many people had ice boxes in their homes. Ice wagons delivered ice once or twice a week. In the nineteenth century, engineers figured out how to cool gases and pump cold air through pipes. Soon, train cars, trucks, meat-packing plants, and dairy farmers were using refrigeration to get more fresh foods to market safely. In the 1920s, household refrigerators began to replace ice boxes. By the 1950s, nearly 90 percent of urban households owned a refrigerator. Today, the refrigerator is one of the most important devices for keeping food safe.

Despite advances such as these, people continued to suffer and die from diseases caused by harmful microbes lurking in their food and drink. Throughout history, large groups of people have fallen prey to the same sickness at the same time. This is called an outbreak. Often, outbreaks occur when a group's water supply becomes contaminated with disease-causing microbes. Cholera is one such disease, caused by certain strains of the *Vibrio* bacteria found in human feces. When communities are hit by heavy rains or floodwaters their sewer systems containing human waste can mix with the fresh water supply. The *Vibrio* bacteria then pass into the water and multiply. People drink the water and become sick. Without fresh supplies of clean water, people infected with cholera can die from dehydration. Cholera outbreaks have not occurred in the United States, nor in most of Europe for several decades, but outbreaks continue to be a problem today in Russia, India, Latin America, and Africa.

Other outbreaks occur when people eat contaminated food such as ergot-contaminated rye or *E. coli*-contaminated beef. Still other food-borne illnesses occur when infected people handle food, especially raw food such as salad greens. **Typhoid** fever, from a strain of *Salmonella* bacteria, and the Hepatitis A virus are transmitted this way.

FOOD LAWS

Once Pasteur and other scientists studied how microbes affect food, citizens began demanding that governments help protect food. In 1862, President Abraham Lincoln founded the United States Department of Agriculture (USDA), which he called the "People's Department." At the time, nearly half the nation's workers were farm workers and they needed good information about healthy farm practices. Today, the USDA watches over the nation's forests, agriculture, health, nutrition, and drinking water. It is responsible for the safety of meat and poultry. Agents regularly inspect meat and poultry processing plants for cleanliness. President Lincoln also appointed a chemist to the USDA. That office has since become today's Food and Drug Administration (FDA). The FDA regulates food and medication and looks after the public health. The agency conducts tests, sets standards, and enforces laws for medication, food, and food processing (except meat and poultry).

In 1906, American author Upton Sinclair wrote a novel called *The Jungle* about the terrible workplace conditions of Chicago's meat-packing plants. His book was read widely and people were outraged at the filthy methods used to slaughter and package meat for sale as food. The public outcry forced the U.S. Government to enact the Pure Food and Drug Act. This act set up guidelines for activities such as workplace cleanliness, worker hand-washing, refrigeration, pasteurization,

Typhoid Mary

....

Typhoid is a dangerous food- and water-borne illness still found in many parts of the world. It is spread by the *Salmonella typhi* bacteria, and affects 17 million people each year with high fevers, headaches, nausea, rashes, and sometimes causes death. It rarely strikes in the United States anymore, due to modern advances in **sanitation** and medication. But in this country in the late nineteenth and early twentieth centuries, typhoid fever was a fearsome killer.

In 1884, a young Irish woman named Mary Mallon immigrated to the United States. She was a fiercely independent person and an excellent cook. Her specialty was homemade peach ice cream. She was popular and accepted many different job offers and frequently moved from family to family, community to community. But as she moved, sickness and death followed her. Mary was a healthy woman. But, unknown to everyone, including herself, she carried the deadly typhoid bacteria in her system. *Salmonella typhi* bacteria lived in Mary's intestines. Without frequent and thorough hand washing, Mary unknowingly allowed the bacteria to migrate to her hard-working fingers and into the food.

Mary's special ice cream was the silent enemy. The *Salmonella* fed greedily on the rich milk fat and multiplied. And because ice cream is not cooked, the bacteria were never killed. Whenever she left a home, she left behind a trail of sick people and sometimes, dead bodies.

One homeowner decided to investigate an outbreak. He hired a sanitary engineer to look for clues. The engineer soon came to suspect Mary Mallon. The engineer tracked Mary's work history. In seven of the last eight homes that she had cooked in, he found people sick with typhoid fever. He confronted her, but Mary refused to believe him. How could she pass along the disease if she herself were not sick? The engineer asked the Health Department to get involved. Public health officials tested her stool samples and found that she did indeed carry the typhoid bacteria. They tried to cure her, but their efforts failed. They even quarantined her—separating her from other people to prevent infection.

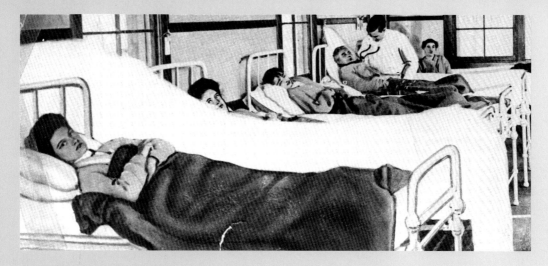

Mary Mallon rests in bed during one of her periods of quarantine.

But Mary continued cooking. Finally, they sought help from the law. New York City courts insisted that Mary Mallon stop working as a cook. They forced her into a hospital for people with infectious diseases. She did not believe she was guilty and was outraged.

After several years in confinement, Mary was allowed to leave the hospital. She needed to work and had promised not to cook again, so she tried working as a laundress. But Mary earned more money cooking, so she changed her name to Mary Brown and started cooking for a hospital in New York City. Before long, twenty five hospital patients were sick with typhoid fever and one patient was dead. Mary was recaptured and sent back to the hospital. She was never released, and died there in 1938. All in all, health officials estimate that she was responsible for more than 1,400 cases of typhoid fever.

Mary Mallon made medical history as one of the first healthy carriers of the typhoid bacteria in the United States. She also made social history with her forceful and determined personality. Today, if people describe someone as a "Typhoid Mary" they mean that person changes jobs frequently, and brings catastrophe and doom along with her.

and healthier animal care. In 1946, the Centers for Disease Control (CDC) was formed to study and control infectious diseases. Among its many duties, the CDC investigates individual cases of food-borne illnesses as well as major outbreaks. Today in the United States, there are numerous federal, state, and local government public health agencies that oversee the safety of food and are dedicated to controlling and preventing the spread of disease.

TODAY'S SCIENCE

Public health officials today say that their work is part detective work, part science, and part high technology. In the past century, many food-borne diseases have been studied. Improved food handling methods have been established. Researchers have developed medication and preventative **vaccines** that defend people against numerous infectious diseases.

But the microbes still exist and newer, more powerful microbes are evolving. "We live in a world full of microbes," says Dr. Howard Markel, author of the book, *When Germs Travel*. In other parts of the world, especially in underdeveloped countries, (countries where there is much poverty and a lack of modern technological advances), food- and water-borne diseases erupt more often, generally because of inadequate sanitation and water systems. Dr. Markel points out that every day, airplanes, trucks, trains, and ships transport people, plants, animals, and food around the globe. The microbes travel, too.

Many coastal communities in the United States suffer outbreaks of food- or water-borne illness when ships empty water and waste overboard. Germs infect the plants, fish, and shellfish. Later, when people eat the contaminated fish and seafood, they can become ill. When an outbreak occurs, public health officials try to discover the cause, find a cure, or develop methods to prevent the outbreak from happening again.

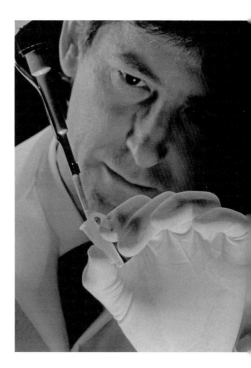

The USDA and other government agencies use different techniques to develop quicker tests for dangerous microbes, such as Hepatitis A and *Listeria*.

In 1992, hundreds of people became sick in Louisiana, Maryland, Mississippi, and North Carolina. At the time, each patient was treated for a single case of food poisoning. No one realized an outbreak was happening. Doctors took stool samples from their patients and sent them to laboratories to be examined. They also took food histories from their patients, asking, "What have you eaten in the last few days?" Many of the doctors reported their patients' symptoms to local public health workers, who then sent the information to the CDC. As CDC officials researched their databases, they discovered that all of these unrelated people had eaten oysters recently. Also, lab tests showed that all of the affected people had the same foreign virus in their stool samples. Further investigation tracked the oysters to a commercial oyster bed in Louisiana. Then they talked to local fishermen. Two of the fishermen reported being sick and vomiting over the side of the boat. In the vomit was a new virus, later to be called a norovirus. The virus had spread to the oyster beds where the oysters absorbed the virus, but were not affected by it. When the oysters were harvested and sold to restaurants, there was no visible sign that a toxic virus was present. Were it not for the fact gathering being done by CDC researchers and the persist-ent efforts of local health care workers, the virus could have continued to spread. In this outbreak, hundreds of people became ill and thousands of bushels of oysters were lost, all because two men were infected with a microscopic virus.

In 1993, a tragic outbreak of *E. coli* 0157:H7 sickened more than seven hundred people in four states, killed four children, and seriously disabled many others. The cause was contaminated hamburger meat. Cattle used for food are crowded together in feedlots, railroad cars, and packing plants before they are slaughtered. The animals step in their feces, and often their hides become contaminated. The infection can pass through to the meat when the animals are slaughtered. Usually only the outer layer of the meat is contaminated, and cooking will destroy the bacteria. But hamburger is ground up, so the germs are mixed throughout the meat. In this outbreak, a large shipment of contaminated ground meat had been distributed to several western states and sold to a fast-food chain. Up to this point, many Americans were used to eating hamburgers that were pink in the center. So no one at first noticed that the hamburgers were under-cooked.

First a girl in San Diego, California, became violently sick with vomiting and bloody diarrhea. Her symptoms worsened and eventually she died. Later in the month, newspapers in Seattle, Washington, reported that unusually high numbers of children were going to the hospital, sick with bloody diarrhea. Investigations began and similar cases in Nevada, California, and Oregon came out into the open. Local hospitals and public health workers shared their lab tests and information with federal researchers. The investigators tracked the infection to the contaminated, under-cooked hamburger being sold by the fast-food chain. By not cooking the burgers thoroughly, the bacteria in the center were not being killed. Young children were the worst affected. People were angry and upset and called for safer foods. The government enacted new food safety laws and regulations. Restaurants followed stricter guidelines for cooking meat. But *E. coli* is not just in hamburger and safety is required when handling any type of food or beverage. Unpasteurized apple juice contaminated with *E. coli* bacteria caused another outbreak three years later.

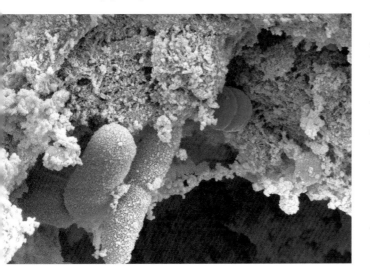

This computer scan shows *E coli* infecting a sample of under-cooked hamburger.

Outbreaks of food-borne illnesses continue to be in the news. There have been parasite infections in raspberries from Guatemala, *Salmonella* poisoning in melons from Mexico, botulism in improperly stored baked potatoes, and many more incidents.

Dr. Elsa Murano of the USDA, said recently, "We have the best food production and processing system in the world, providing consumers with the most abundant and safest food supply. However, over the last few years we have seen evidence that . . . this system is not perfect. Food safety continues to be a serious matter and one that, if not continually addressed, can lead to tragic events."

Everyone has a role to play in preventing food-borne illness. Consumers, restaurant employees, and grocery store workers need to keep their hands, food, kitchens, and storage areas clean. Farmers must use clean water on their crops and refrigerate their produce properly. Animal handlers and meat processors need to carefully follow government guidelines for cleanliness and safety. Researchers should continue developing medication to cure food-borne illnesses and methods to prevent new outbreaks. Health-care workers must examine their patients thoroughly and report useful information to public health officials. Newspaper, radio, and television reporters should accurately inform the public whenever food-borne outbreaks occur. Preventing food-borne illnesses is a shared responsibility. With research, prompt and thorough health care, accurate information, and everyday common sense, people around the world can work together to keep the food they eat safe.

4

TREATING AND COPING WITH A FOOD-BORNE ILLNESS

Many people have had a food-borne illness without knowing it. The illnesses are common and most cases are minor. When people suffer mild symptoms, they usually recover at home, in one to two days, and are not likely to report their illness. But some cases are critical, even deadly, and require serious medical attention. Medical experts say that while there are hundreds of different causes for food-borne illnesses, there may be hundreds more unknown causes. Because of the large variety, diagnosing or detecting a food-borne illness can be difficult. Typical symptoms include a sudden bout of nausea, vomiting, abdominal cramps, and diarrhea. When these symptoms last longer than 48 hours, or when they worsen to include fever, chills, bloody diarrhea, dehydration, and nervous system disorders, it is important to contact a health-care provider.

HOME TREATMENT

The most common type of treatment occurs at home. People with mild cases of food poisoning undergo short periods of vomiting and diarrhea. Generally, these symptoms do not last longer than two days. The greatest problem with these symptoms is dehydration. Dehydration is a lack of fluids in the body. To treat dehydration, a patient should take frequent sips of clear fluids, such as water or very diluted sports drinks. People should avoid sugary or caffeinated drinks such as soda, tea, coffee, or full-strength sports drinks. Once a patient stops vomiting and feeling nauseous, he or she can eat simple, non-greasy, and non-spicy foods, such as

Abdominal cramps are a typical symptom of most food-borne illnesses.

rice, bread, or a non-citrus fruit. "We call it the BRAT diet," says one hospital nurse, "that stands for Bananas, Rice, Applesauce, and Toast."

VISITING A HEALTH-CARE PROVIDER

While most food-borne illnesses can be treated at home, there are many situations that call for more medical attention.

Reasons to contact a medical professional include:

- vomiting and diarrhea lasting more than two days
- fever
- nervous system problems such as slurred speech, double vision, trouble swallowing, or muscle weakness
- or if the patients are frail and elderly, three years old or younger, or have a weakened immune system.

When a patient must take medication for a different health condition, he or she should contact a health-care professional right away. The patient's vomiting can prevent him or her from keeping the medication down.

If a health-care provider feels that symptoms are worsening, he or she will want to examine the patient in person. During a medical examination for a food-borne illness, a patient should expect to provide as many details as possible about symptoms and about the foods eaten in the recent past. The medical practitioner will also do a physical exam that includes checking blood pressure, pulse, breathing rate, and temperature. He or she will also examine the patient's abdomen and check for signs of dehydration. The patient may be asked for blood, urine, or stool samples. These samples are sent to a laboratory. There, technicians can sometimes determine the type of microbe that is doing the damage. A few bacteria infections can be treated with **antibiotics.** This medication does not work for a virus infection, however. The health-care practitioner may suggest other treatments, possibly including medications that reduce fever or stop vomiting and diarrhea.

HOSPITAL CARE

Though rare, some cases of food-borne illness are extremely dangerous. People experiencing abnormal symptoms should go to the nearest hospital's emergency room and seek immediate medical care. Abnormal symptoms include:

- dizziness or fainting
- a fever over 101 degrees Fahrenheit
- swelling of the stomach
- yellowing of the eyes or skin
- swelling of joints
- rashes on skin
- blood in vomit or in diarrhea
- very dark urine
- no urine
- or trouble breathing and swallowing.

These symptoms are all signs of serious food poisoning and without treatment, they can lead to nervous system or kidney damage or even death.

At the hospital, a patient will be examined. **Ultrasounds,** scans, and rectal exams may be performed to inspect the intestinal tract and to check for any breaks or tears where bacteria could be escaping. For cases of food poisoning, an X ray is generally performed on the abdominal area. The X ray provides doctors with a picture of a person's internal organs. A biopsy is a procedure that collects a tissue sample from the patient's infected organs, using a special needle. The tissue is examined under a microscope to try to determine the nature of the toxin.

A patient may need to receive fluids by IV. IV is short for intravenous, meaning in the vein. A needle is placed in a patient's vein, and tubes are connected to it. The tubes deliver necessary fluids directly to the bloodstream to help rehydrate the patient. If a patient has eaten a very toxic substance such as poisonous mushrooms, contaminated shellfish, or foods contaminated with pesticides, he or she may undergo stomach pumping to remove the toxins.

COPING

The average food-borne illness lasts two days. During those two days, a person can expect to suffer vomiting, nausea, cramps, and diarrhea. The patient will probably dislike the idea of eating food for awhile, especially foods similar to those that caused the illness. "Pizza! What kid doesn't like pizza? Not me. Not for years," explains Ashley, who as a little girl suffered food poisoning after eating a contaminated slice of pizza at a fair. Once patients have stopped vomiting or having diarrhea, they will continue to feel weak. Their stomach and intestines will feel tender and sore for a few days. Drinking water mixed with non-citrus, unsweetened fruit juice is the best way to start feeling better. Patients should begin eating slowly, in very small amounts. The best foods to reintroduce are bananas, applesauce, whole-grain breads, crackers, pasta, and rice. After all the symptoms have passed, patients should rest and plan to miss one or two more days of school or work. Avoiding vigorous physical activity is also wise.

People who have suffered serious, life-threatening episodes of food poisoning will have a long recovery period. Some may be left with a chronic condition for the rest of their lives. Some permanent disabilities that have come as a result of food-borne illnesses are kidney disease, diabetes (disease of the pancreas), arthritis (joint pain), paralysis, seizures, or the immune system-nervous system disease, Guillain-Barre syndrome. When suffering from one or more of these various conditions, patients will be in fragile health, may require daily medication, will need to limit their activities, and may experience pain every day.

Filing a Complaint

Chances are if you have suffered from a food-borne illness, someone else who has eaten the same food as you will also become sick. In many cases, you can help stop the spread of disease by talking to an adult about notifying the local Health Department. When you do, public health officials act quickly to find the source of the contamination. So if you become sick with an episode of food poisoning, think about the foods you have eaten over the last 24 to 48 hours.

With your help, public health agencies can prevent a serious outbreak. But it is important to speak to an adult, such as a parent or other guardian, before contacting these agencies. Once you have discussed these issues, here are some tips for filing a complaint about food poisoning:

• If you have eaten contaminated meat, poultry, or eggs, call the USDA Meat and Poultry Hotline at 1-800-535-4555

• If you have eaten contaminated fish or seafood, call the FDA Seafood Hotline at 1-800-332-4010

• If you believe food from a particular restaurant has made you ill, call your local Health Department. You will find the number in the government section of the telephone book. Usually these pages are blue. The sections of government listed are separated into federal, state, county, and city.

• If you have eaten spoiled food purchased from a store, call the store and call your local Health Department. Keep any packaging you can for identification. For best results, try to provide the following information and do the following things:

> • Brand name and product name
> • Manufacturer and distributor
> • Name of store where purchased
> • Date purchased
> • Description of package
> • Any bar code markings

> • Any dates or codes stamped on package
> • If you have found a foreign object in food, wrap everything in plastic and keep it cold to preserve it
> • Keep any uneaten food to test for contaminants

PREVENTION

The best way to fight a food-borne illness is to prevent it. Experts call the four basic areas of prevention: Cook, Clean, Separate, and Chill.

Cook

Foods, especially meat, eggs, and poultry, need to be cooked thoroughly. Carefully read the directions on food labels before cooking. Picking up the habit of using a meat thermometer

to test for doneness is a good idea. With an adult's help, this is an easy task to do. When properly cooked, the center of a hamburger should have a temperature of at least 165 degrees Fahrenheit. Chicken should be at 180 degrees F. Never eat ground beef or poultry that is pink inside. Heat hot dogs until they are hot and steaming. Leftovers, hot dogs, or prepared foods should be heated to a temperature of 165 degrees Fahrenheit. If you are using a microwave oven, stop the oven, stir the food, and re-start the oven, so that the food is heated evenly. Cook eggs until they are firm and not runny. If uncooked

A meat thermometer is used to be sure that meats, casseroles, and other baked foods have been thoroughly heated at temperatures that will kill all harmful bacteria.

eggs are used in a recipe, such as cookies, do not taste the raw dough, wait until the cookies are baked.

It is important to keep cooked foods hot. Do not let cooked foods sit out for more than two hours. They should not sit for more than one hour if the temperature of the air is 90 degrees. Bacteria thrive at room temperature. Students bringing cooked foods in a lunch bag to school should be careful that the food stays hot. These foods should be stored in an insulated bottle or thermos, in an insulated lunch box. Here is a neat trick to help keep food in insulated bottles warm: Before putting the hot food in the insulated bottle, have an adult pour boiling water in the bottle and let it stand for a few minutes. Empty the water and add the hot food. Close the lid tightly and do not open it until you are ready to eat.

Clean

Always wash your hands before preparing food. Simply rinsing with water is not enough to get rid of bacteria and other germs. Use warm, soapy water and scrub the palms, the tops of hands, and between the fingers. Many teachers ask their students to time the length of their hand-washing by singing a little song to themselves like *Happy Birthday* or the *Alphabet Song* all the way through. Dry your hands completely with a clean towel or paper towel. Do not wipe hands on clothing since there are germs on the clothing. "Remember," says Christine Fulgham, a home economics teacher, "germs like the same conditions as we do—they like water, warmth, and air."

When preparing food, be sure that the kitchen surfaces are clean. Wash fruits and vegetables that will be eaten raw very carefully. Wash knives and cutting boards with hot, soapy water after use. With adult supervision, it is a good idea to rinse cutting boards with a bleach-and-water solution. Do not place backpacks, clothes, shoes, coats, or other similar items on the counter. Keep all kitchen counters, shelves, refrigerators, and freezers clean.

Separate

Separate foods from one another to avoid cross-contamination. Never place cooked food or food to be eaten raw on a surface that held raw meat, eggs, or poultry. Also, do not use the same cutting board or utensil (stirring spoon, knife, or fork) for raw meat, eggs, and poultry with foods that are ready to eat.

Avoid mixing and storing unlike foods, especially protein foods, such as meat, eggs, cheese, and milk. For example, using the same knife in the mayonnaise jar that is used in the mustard jar, or using the same spoon for both sour cream and salsa can cause cross-contamination and encourage spoiling. Cross-contamination causes the most food-borne illnesses. When food handlers in restaurants, delis, or cafeterias touch uncooked meats, poultry, and eggs, and then, without washing their hands, touch salads or raw fruits and vegetables, viruses and bacteria are spread. Always wash your hands after handling raw meats, eggs, and poultry, and before touching other foods.

Chill

Proper food storage is key to preventing a food-borne illness. At room temperature, some bacteria can double in quantity every twenty minutes. Cool temperatures block germs from multiplying. Refrigerators should be set to 40 degrees or below, and freezers to at least 0 degrees. When food shopping, buy perishable (foods that spoil without refrigeration) last. At home, put those foods away first.

Set refrigerators at a temperature of 40 degrees F or below and do not leave refrigerator or freezer doors open any longer than necessary.

If stored in the refrigerator for two days, poultry, fish, and other meats should either be cooked or frozen. When thawing frozen foods, do so slowly in the refrigerator or place the food in cold water in the sink. Leaving frozen food to thaw at room temperature exposes the outer portion of the food to dangerous temperatures allowing bacteria to grow rapidly. Always cover or wrap foods to keep air out. Most cooked leftovers should be eaten within four days, or thrown out. Return perishable foods to the refrigerator immediately after use.

Summer is a great time for picnics, but a challenging time for food safety. Warm temperatures create the perfect environment for germs to grow. Fill coolers with several inches of ice cubes, or a block of ice. Keep lunch meat, cooked meats, salads, and sandwiches cold. If it is very hot, and the outing is a long one, it is a good idea to carry along two coolers. Keep perishable foods in one, and beverages in the other. The beverage cooler will usually be opened more frequently—causing the air inside to warm faster. The other cooler, if kept closed, will keep food colder longer.

When school starts, the next challenge is keeping the contents of a school lunch safe. Insulated lunch boxes are best for this, but if one is not available, use two lunch bags. Putting something cold in the lunch will keep sandwiches, fruits, and vegetables fresh. Freezing a juice box and packing it in the lunch box is a great way to have a fresh meal and a

Traveling Tips

For many people, one of the most satisfying parts of travel in foreign countries is sampling and tasting new foods. But beware that food poisoning can happen when it is least expected. Regional foods rarely make locals sick, but travelers are not used to the different microbes that thrive in other parts of the world, and can suddenly find their vacation spoiled by a bout of food poisoning. Travel and health experts offer this advice: "Cook it, wash it, peel it, or forget it." What this means is that to be safe, food should be cooked and eaten while it is very hot. Look for busy restaurants that appear to have clean kitchens and careful staff. Be sure that foods are washed thoroughly in clean water. Keep your own hands clean, too. Fruits and vegetables should be avoided, unless they have thick skins, such as oranges or mangoes. These can be peeled with a clean knife or hands. Thin-skinned fruits and vegetables, such as tomatoes or lettuce, absorb microbes in the soil in which they were grown. These microbes can make a traveler sick. Milk, cold meats, mayonnaise, puddings, and ice cream are often foods to "forget."

Water is a frequent source of a food-borne illness when traveling or hiking. Common microbes found in contaminated water are *E. coli,* cholera, *Salmonella*, rotavirus, Hepatitis A, polio, *Giardia*, and *Cryptosporidium*. While some of these contaminants can be filtered, killed by heat, or treated with chemicals, no one method of cleansing the water works in all situations. So unless you have no other option, experts recommend that people just avoid drinking any local water and instead drink bottled water, canned juice, hot coffee or tea, or bottled soda.

In foreign countries, travelers should avoid ice cubes, unless they have been prepared with purified water. Even the smallest drop of contaminated water can make a person sick. Remember to use only purified water for rinsing foods and brushing teeth. If you do get sick, chances are that the infection will run its course in a few days and symptoms will be mild. Drink lots of clear fluids and rest. However, if symptoms worsen, or a fever persists, seek professional medical care.

cold drink at lunchtime. Including a freezer gel pack in the lunch box, or a small, plastic container filled with water that has been frozen overnight will keep sandwiches fresh and tasty. An insulated bottle to store milk or juice is a good way to keep drinks chilled. At school, keep lunch boxes in a cool place, away from heaters or sunny windows. Discard any perishable food not eaten at lunch time. It is not a healthy snack for later!

INSPECTION

It is a good idea to inspect food. If the food is discolored, moldy, has an odor, or if the texture is not right—for example, soggy instead of crisp—throw it away, and do not eat it. Check the dates on food labels, especially protein foods, which spoil quickly, such as milk, eggs, fish, meats, soft cheese, and sour cream. Never consume food from torn or leaking packages. If a can is dented, or bulging at the top, throw it out. (A bloated or bulging can is often a sign that bacteria or other germs are growing inside. They are the ones releasing the air that makes the can bulge!)

Germs that cause disease cannot be seen by the naked eye, so it is very important that people are aware that microbes exist all around them. It is impossible to avoid all microbes all the time. But following safety steps for cleanliness, food handling, cooking, and storing is the smartest way to avoid a food-borne illness.

GLOSSARY

bacteria—Microscopic organisms composed of a single cell.

botulism—A food-borne illness caused by *Clostridium* bacteria.

Campylobacter—A group of related bacteria. Some strains found in poultry, unpasteurized milk and juice, fresh produce, and contaminated water cause food-borne illness.

chronic—Lasting a long time, ongoing, or happening again and again.

Clostridium—A type of bacteria that releases toxins that can be harmful or deadly to animals, including humans. *Clostridium* causes botulism.

contamination—The presence of harmful microorganisms in food or water.

dehydration—In humans, the loss of necessary body fluids and chemicals.

diarrhea—Loose or watery bowel movements, usually caused by a food-borne infection or irritation of the digestive system.

E. coli—(scientific name *Escherichia coli*) A group of related bacteria. Some types are harmful to humans. *E.coli* can be found in raw or undercooked beef, unpasteurized milk, and raw vegetables.

feces—Bodily waste that is pushed out of the body after digestion. Also called stool.

germ—A term commonly used to describe bacteria, viruses, parasites, and other microorganisms that cause illnes.

Giardia—A parasitic microscopic organism that lives in animal intestines and can cause food-borne illnesses.

Guillain-Barre syndrome—A neurological condition that causes nerve damage, numbness, and paralysis.

Hepatitis A—A virus that sickens the liver and is transmitted in food by unsafe food handling.

host—The organism upon which a parasite preys.

immune system—A complex network of specialized cells, tissues, and organs that defends the body against illness.

Listeria—A group of related bacteria. Some strains cause serious food-borne illness. *Listeria* can survive very cold temperatures and are found in raw meat, unpasteurized milk and soft cheeses, and raw vegetables.

microbes—Very tiny living things—often called microorganisms.

microorganisms—Very small organisms that can only be seen with a microscope. These include bacteria, viruses, fungi, plants, and microscopic parasitic creatures.

nausea—An uneasy sensation in the stomach that may develop into an intense urge to vomit.

parasites—Microorganisms that live, grow, and feed on or within another living organism.

pasteurization—The process discovered by Louis Pasteur that kills pathogens in food, usually by heat.

pathogens—Disease-causing organisms. Viruses and bacteria can be pathogens.

peristalsis—A rhythm of tightening and relaxing of muscles and organs to move food through the digestive system and out of the body.

Salmonella—A group of related bacteria. Several strains of *Salmonella* can be found in poultry and eggs and may cause food borne-illnesses in humans.

Shigella—A type of bacteria that creates a toxin and causes a food borne-illness.

sanitation—The process of killing or removing germs and waste.

seizures—Electrical misfires in the brain that cause uncontrollable movement or unconsciousness.

toxoplasma—A type of parasite that can cause food-borne illnesses.

typhoid—A serious infection having symptoms of gastrointestinal illness, fever, and severe headache caused by *Salmonella typhi*.

ultrasound—A medical device that takes an image using sound waves.

vaccine—A substance made of parts of an infectious organism used in medicine to help protect the body from the disease caused by that organism.

virus—A microorganism that causes many diseases and illness in humans, animals, and plants.

FIND OUT MORE

Organizations

Food Safety and Inspection Service (FSIS), US Department of Agriculture (USDA) Meat and Poultry Hotline:

(888) MPHotline (1-888-674-6854)

(800) 256-7072 (TDD/TTY)

This government hotline is run by nutritionists and food specialists who answer citizens' questions about food safety.

Center for Science in the Public Interest

1875 Connecticut Ave NW Suite 300

Washington, DC 20009

(202) 332-9110

http://cspinet.org/foodsafety

This organization represents the citizens' interest in food safety to the government. It also educates the public on improving food safety and nutritional quality of food.

Environmental Protection Agency (EPA) Safe Drinking Water Hotline

(800) 426-4791

The EPA provides information about drinking water standards and safety.

Food and Drug Administration (FDA) Seafood Hotline

(800) FDA-4010

This government hotline provides advice on buying, storing and preparing seafood. Seafood alerts are announced at the beginning of each phone call.

United States Department of Agriculture / Food and Drug Administration (USDA/FDA) Foodborne Illness Education and Information Center

10301 Baltimore Boulevard, Room 304

Beltsville, MD 20705

(301) 504-5719

http://www.nal.usda.gov/foodborne

This government center provides food-borne illness prevention information to individuals, schools, and food workers.

Books

Gordon, Sharon. *Food Safety*. Danbury, CT: Children's Press, 2001.

Isle, Mick. *Everything You Need To Know About Food Poisoning*.
New York: Rosen Publishing, 2001.

Silverstein, Alvin. *What are Germs?* Danbury, CT: Franklin Watts,
2002.

Woodward, John. *Our Food*. New York: Gareth Stevens Publisher,
1997.

Web Sites

The American Medical Association
http://www.ama-assn.org/go/foodborne

Centers for Disease Control and Prevention
http://www.cdc.gov/foodsafety/cme.htm

ABOUT THE AUTHOR

Ruth Bjorklund lives on Bainbridge Island in Washington state. Along with her husband and two children, she enjoys traveling, hiking, and sailing trips. In every one of their adventures, she reminds her family to practice their food safety rules!